The City and the Child

The City and the Child

Aleš Debeljak

Translated by
Christopher Merrill and the author

White Pine Press · Buffalo, New York

WHITE PINE PRESS
P.O. Box 236, Buffalo, New York 14201

Publication of this book was made possible, in part,
by grants from the National Endowment for the Arts,
the New York State Council on the Arts,
the Trubar Foundation, and the Chrysopolae Foundation..

Acknowledgments:
Grateful acknowledgment is made to the following publications
in which some of the translations first appeared:
Harvard Review, Seneca Review, Tin House, Trafika, and *Verse.*

Book design: Elaine LaMattina

Printed and bound in the United States of America

1 3 5 7 9 10 8 6 4 2

Library of Congress Cataloging-in-Publication Data

Debeljak, Aleš, 1961–
[Mesto in otrok. English]
The city and the child / Aleš Debeljak ; translated by Christopher Merrill. and the author.
p. cm. — (Terra incognita series ; 5)
ISBN 1-877727-99-7 (alk. paper)
I. Merrill, Christopher. II. Title III. Series: Terra incognita.
(Fredonia, N.Y.) ; vol. 5.
PG1919.14.E28M4713 1999
891.8'415—dc21   99–43486
CIP

For both of you

Contents

Second Baptism

Interpretation of Love

Young Muse

Homecoming

Translator's Introduction

The City and the Child is a fine example of what Yeats in another context called "Speech after long silence": a hymn, that is, to possibility, in the wake of a devastating loss. What prompted the Irish poet's lyric was the recognition in old age that he could speak again from the heart to Maud Gonne, his lost love: "Bodily decrepitude is wisdom," he laments, even as he recalls the innocence in which they loved each other. A different form of innocent love animates Aleš Debeljak's new collection of poems: for the Slovenian poet it was the birth of a child, coupled with the breakup of Yugoslavia, that spurred him into song—forty-two irregular sonnets, to be precise. And his daughter, "a new source," is the muse of these poems, composed in the fall of 1995, as the war ground to a halt. This, then, is "a chronicle of pain," tempered by a new and exuberant love: "the seed, the blossom, and the fruit."

An extended poetic silence preceded *The City and the Child*. Although Debeljak wrote no poems between 1990 and 1995, a silence commensurate with Yugoslavia's slide into war, he carried on an active literary life, publishing books of cultural criticism, essays, translations, and weekly columns for Slovenia's largest daily newspaper. Nor was his poetic silence out of character. His is a most unusual method of writing: after a long fallow period, poetically speaking, he will produce an entire book of poems in a matter of months. Each book is divided into seven cycles, in which images recur and reinforce one another. Indeed the whole of any Debeljak collection is larger than the sum of its parts. Nor is his poetry immune to the currents of politics and history. His last volume, for example, *Anxious Moments*, a collection of prose poems, contained phrases and imagery that prefigured the

Third Balkan War—military hospitals and convoys, razed villages, "white phosphorous lighting the passion in soldiers' eyes." And *The City and the Child* is notable for the ways in which it records and transforms the awful legacy of the war that claimed 200,000 lives and dislocated millions more.

The sonnet holds a singular place in Slovenian letters. In 1834, France Prešeren, Slovenia's national poet, published a famous wreath of sonnets, which laid the foundation for the literary tradition of a people then on the verge of acquiring a national consciousness. His sonnets are almost as important to his countrymen as his "Toast to Freedom," a poem published in 1848, during "the springtime of nations," which became Slovenia's national anthem when it won its independence from Yugoslavia in 1991, after waging a brief war of secession. It is no coincidence, then, that Debeljak, who burst onto the Yugoslav literary scene in 1985 with a collection of sonnets, *The Names of the Dead*, has returned to the form for *The City and the Child*. This is at once a meditation on the conjunction of war and fatherhood and a commentary on a national literary tradition. Debeljak's post-Yugoslav sonnets rely on internal rhyme instead of end rhyme, and they are generally about three feet longer than the pentameter norm— effects I have tried to maintain in these English versions.

This translation was begun in Ljubljana, Slovenia, in the fall of 1997 and completed the following spring in Connecticut. The poet provided me with literal English versions of the poems, checked over by his American wife, Erica, from which I wrote the first draft of *The City and the Child*. Debeljak and I then worked through the mail, over the telephone, and during a visit he made to my home to bring the poems to fruition. My thanks to him and to Erica not only for their tireless efforts to answer my questions but also for their hospitality. My thanks as well to Domenick DiPasquale and Sandy Rouse for providing me with a U.S. Information Agency travel grant to Slovenia. And a translation award from the Slovenian Cultural Ministry enabled me to finish this book in a timely fashion.

—Christopher Merrill

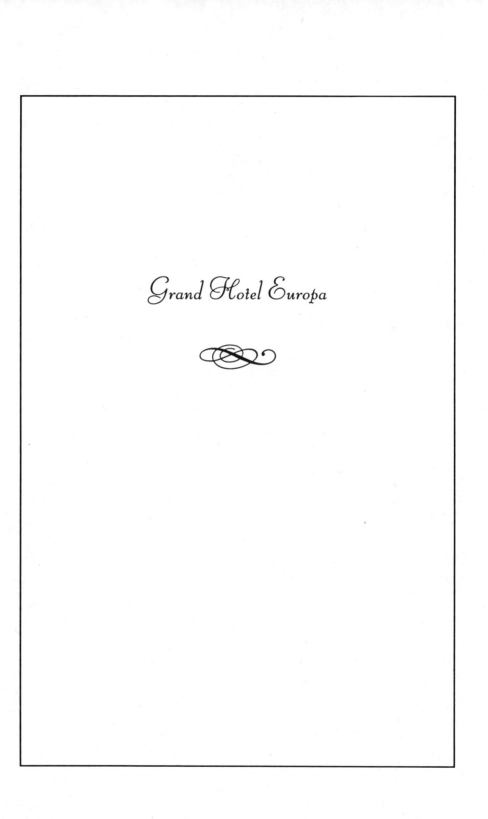

Grand Hotel Europa

Faces in Front of the Wall

Humble is the charity of early mornings. Everything that happens then
must happen: to you, to me, to the whole world. Temptation
is great indeed: we gaze, enchanted, as a fire's eternal glow
melts the columns of cathedrals, a virgin's slumber, and the hidden

spring of a toy. We watch, motionless, as in a tranquil family crypt.
Each of us, I think, is already doomed. We're silent. What else could we do?
Like a stunned witness in a country when it was still
a country. It lives on, exiled into an image which won't let us sleep.

Day and night quiver in our pupils. Do we kneel, hoping the storm will take
pity on us and bring a mother's gentle forgiveness? That it will blur the line
between the altar and the offering? I guess, I know:

there's no greater mistake. Embers cover the fire screen. Even the blood
spilling down a girl's hip has lost its taste. It doesn't smell like plowed soil
crumbling in our fingers. In vain we try: we're less than a footnote.

Weather Forecast

A spring shower rushes over the sunken monarchy. Will it ever end?
The rhythm striking the window lulls me into a deep coma.
I hand myself over to silence and flow into damp soil
so that in a year or two I can live in a cloud: my true sanctuary.

A faithful horse takes a Cossack toward town. Perhaps the rider
doesn't know it yet: his death, like all languages erased from the earth,
will be laid at invisible feet. Even greater adventurers await the end
of the natural cycle. But it's not up to me to judge.

I can only rain on the crying child in diapers, on carts
and burnt skyscrapers, on the tobacco smuggling route. I rain:
I don't ask where the widows in black have gone. I cover everything,

like a transparent varnish. I rain. On a balance, on coffins
used for shelter. I rain down on the spine of the boy who will stand
before a line of sturdy soldiers, give an order, and the line will shudder.

Grand Hotel Europa

The Carline thistles wither in the vase on the shelf. No man's land
beckons me. I'm guilty because I won't forget. That would be easy
like the course of a hasty flock cutting the sky. I lean against the window,
as others have before me. The taste of fruit, the nude woman

who visits me in dreams: nothing I touch surprises me anymore.
And the harmony of a still life doesn't help. A different pain
blinds me. I want to share it with someone. But with whom? If I
whisper it alone into the night, its echo won't find its way back. If

we all speak it vanishes, like a copper engraving in a blast furnace.
But I cannot renounce it. Mine is the fear of the fugitive who couldn't hide
in this cheap room. When the merciless god covers the window frame only

the mirror will preserve their faces. I'll lend them my throat to intercept
the barking of dogs and the blare of a hunter's horn. I can't even see myself
anymore, yet I must sing for them to find peace in my song, finally united.

Grapes of Mercy

Come back to lighten our soul and let the contagious steam
evaporate in the extra verse. Come back to spin the axis,
to weight and center bedrooms again. Here, where the union
of animals and clay depends on a weak hunch, here you mean more

than water to a captive muttering the Pater Noster. Come back
to guide our hand with the allure of fruit we don't dare pick.
Without you we cannot distinguish between the seasons, we can
only make wild guesses. The neck is rigid, and storks are flying south.

It's high time: come. Present us with a gift, the key to the future,
to noble nostalgia. It's enough that you exist. Like a fragrance
which doesn't go up in smoke when our first woman leaves us. Solitude

must move you to test us in perfection. Let us be in pain. You'll be with us
like a stain spreading over a clay jar: first a small spot, then a flood
softening the edges until the room gives way under its own weight.

Pastoral

The ornament of frost and jasmine is already crumbling. Before
a tent, a thrush generously scatters psalms across the earth. The day
is almost gone. I have mercy for the future scar, like a letter
in which a private *Iliad* begins. A kiss on the forehead—

I give it lightly: a father moans on his deathbed, the family
has left. One is missing, inspiring black epics. For a long time
he has been marching elsewhere. He surrendered to the spell
of the banner fluttering above the castle. I had wished

that at least the youngest lamb would see the zenith.
But the forms of darkness are everywhere. What could I have done?
I left home like a pilgrim bound for Rome. I departed early.

Had I not gone, my lost brother would not have lifted a hand against me
in a nomadic hallucination. Thus the road is marked with mines and I can
only stutter. No symmetry, no design: an ancient seal cracks imperceptibly.

Mercenaries

The wind has died down in the vineyards on the hills. A moth flaps
against a carbon lamp. Evening draws a feeble breath. A prayer, unheeded,
disappears in the twilight. God remains indifferent. From a distance
we watch the heirs to a mighty throne tremble at the decrees. Dynasties

endlessly rise and fall. North and south, east and west: we serve you
faithfully. The triumphal arch pierces the clouds. It's not mulberry juice
that sticks to our palms. We grip our shields. In a dismembered country
a tangled vine grows in neglect. We can only guess at its suffering. Langobards,

Scythians, masters of Norik: in the name of another's victory we opened
treasuries and skulls, leaving behind us empty caverns. Now we rest.
Our work is done. It won't be easy to begin again.

Our sight, too, has given out. All we can see is the simple order
of things. Not much, less than nothing. We don't even recognize
the face in the puddle when at times it reflects our own image.

Migrations

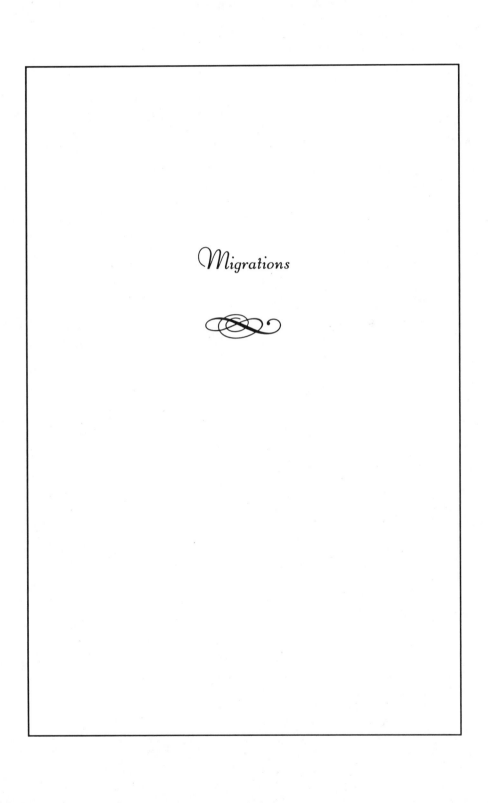

Cosmopolis

for Josip Osti
Sarajevo-Ljubljana

Listen well: is that the trumpet call? The cavalry
rides through history. The shadow of an ancient battle
wants to be the truth again. A distant stairway winds toward a cloud.
Mountains fall, a chalice trembles. Emptiness spills over

the edge. Yet you, miraculously, grow faster than you can be
destroyed. A titmouse will not leave its nest. The west wind
tempts you with redemption in a hollowed loaf of bread
at the Last Supper. A broken toy. More children are missing.

Yet you endure. You interrupt the world's monologue, its endless drone.
You're the flickering snow on the screen, which is always on. The vault
of the universe above you is crystal clear. The rest of us

stare helplessly into the cold prison of the stars. We watch a finger
rise from the flame flickering behind your back, which never consumes you.
And on the arch of the sky the finger writes, tirelessly, "I am."

Migrations

You see everything, everything: the breath of flies, a teapot
whistling, a cartridge recklessly shot off at daybreak, a pattern
on the wallpaper, the gloom of a concert hall, dusty violins left
in haste on the floor, an inscription in the language of the two

prophets who came to the Slavs, things drowning in infinite
light, a scream tearing suddenly across the sky, gleaming metal,
a column of children and women carrying newborn babies, the scent
of basil in a garden, a trickle of plum juice oozing into the rutted

tracks left by retreating armies. Everything. You see graveyards.
And metastases of white-hot pyres. Here the world we know lets out
its final gasp. The ancient order of violence is returning to the hearths.

The magic of words is dying out. And a girls' choir stands in silence.
A trail points east, across a snowy pass. Nothing erases it.
Now you know the bell tolls for you and for us.

The City and the Child

No cry, really, is meaningless. Only when an archangel
appears, like a blue gentian on a mountain slope, do we know,
if only for an instant, our native land. Your Babylonian
moan won't die away. That's why poets never sleep. The task

seems clear now: this will be a chronicle of pain.
The size of a melting glacier. Which floods poppy fields
and villages, targets painted on the portal's slender frieze,
the lush filigree of Turkish silver: each tear deepens you.

You stand on the immovable rock. The world around you crumbles
into the abyss. You drink the water of life, drawn from the mouths
of those who breathe with you. Each morning they come to witness

your rebirth. Like this poem. It won't be long before an avalanche
silences it. But a thousand echoes will spring up in its place. For the love
flowing through your veins is the seed, the blossom, and the fruit.

Metamorphosis of Grass

(on a theme by Ovid)

The grass on a grave grows faster than memory. A green down blanket
hides ankles and palms. And the sapling of guilt planted in the liver
grows like the choir's silence when the cantata ends. It's true:
when this song is over no one will live in its verses.

Longing weighs on me when I open doors. I go from room to room
and across the hills of Galilee, which sense the coming drought.
I confess: I sing sotto voce. The radio drowns me out. Yet something
orders me not to renounce the word. The word which will outlive

this generation. Sharper than salt oozing through the walls
of the heart. I stumble down the overgrown path. If I have to,
I'll take into my arms the animal whimpering in the brambles.

Over lilies I go, past the last man. Through the cruelest months
I wade alone. Not just April: eternity separates me from my brother.
And in the house the carpet turns to hair, like a meadow.

The Imperfect Passion of a Word

Where a flock of starlings should fly—only the emptiness
of air breaks open. Barrels of oil have been burning for a long time.
Hardly an image of paradise, it's true. But not yet hell. Old men
sing lamentations under the ruins of the brick arcades. It's enough

that one solitary child listens to them from a foreign land. The echo
of a ballad gives him strength. Heavy, dark birds glide through
sleep, and in their unbridled lust boys discover light. A razor blade
slices across a young face and tenderness now seems heroic. They say

a draft of a sonnet can't be squeezed out of memory's decay.
Well, perhaps. But that would be a bitter image. I can only say:
silence interests me less than the imperfect passion of a word,

from which a seed explodes into flower. Channeling the delirious
vows of strangers, the century's bodies and souls, into the aqueduct
of language: I know in my blood that this is not in vain.

The Beauty of Failure

for Tomaž Šalamun
at home and abroad

A shimmering comet burns out above the woods and water.
Karst wine ages in noble barrels. You love the sweet torment
of song. You are drawn to a place where you can name
everything. And here the century turns: language

takes no shortcuts. You, who easily revive the sleep
of the unborn, waited, in vain, in a hotel room for the majestic
deer to approach as they did in the past, when you hunted freely,
naked and strong, over the plains of many kingdoms.

You follow morning's first frightening light, which instantly
sobers drunks and changes you into a seer. And yet you doubt
your gift. You did not feel the hush laid across the fur

of deer gathering in herds. Which out of loyalty to you renounced
caves and dens. Which long awaited your turning from hunter
to shepherd so that the Milky Way would once again appear.

Manufacturing Dust

Hunters' Initiation

Through narrow river beds you sail the Danube to the Black Sea.
Hail clatters through the creamy mist, on the tombstones of soldiers
and monks. Under the dome of the boundless empire a hawk
swoops down on its prey, too small to be seen. You sail beyond

canals destroyed by an unknown force, past the monastery
and the vision of paradise promised in ancestral records. You cross
borders lightly, like a smuggler, a fox stealing into sleeping houses.
The governess has bathed the firstborn son for the last time.

Under coats of paint fresh blood glows. Isolated villages pray
for deliverance, for miraculous fire. They refuse to flee.
After sailing for years, the pallor of old age begins to gnaw at you.

Damnation and triumph are last year's snow to you. You advance
on the stone wall of the fortress, which waits for the ritual of history
to be repeated. It, too, will be razed by a child's delicate breath.

Bosnian Elegy

for Miljenko Jergović
Sarajevo-Zagreb

Sing, young poet, touch my burning skin, darkened by long treks
through wild hills to the ends of the world. Don't give up now,
when the gunners' fevered sights are trained on the stained façades
of museums and palaces. They cower silently, like spent reliquaries.

Just list what remains: flocks of swallows twittering under former
arches and campaniles, the eternal wisdom of the French novel
we read in the bomb shelter, the silvery down which disappears
from a baby's earlobes, thunder from the Pannonian plains.

The smell of gunpowder irritates the lungs. We haven't yet crossed
the line. Speak now: the surface of the pool ripples. I don't know
if it will be blessed. Rings glow in the depths. What remains unknown

rejoices. Believe me: I'm ready, sing to me for the last time of the gentle
love of storms, of the mysteries of a woman's shadow and a marble
staircase. Sing, as you sang before your hair turned grey!

Manufacturing Dust

Does a little teardrop sting? Do your loins already ache? Do you
really know the pillar of salt which blooms from helplessness? In vain
you stare at the snow on the TV screen. The false prophet's light
streams by in dazzling carnivals. Yet no one says a word.

The right to choose, you say, the ascetic order you create gliding
across the channels. In fact, the blinding terrors of childhood
rise from that hollow gourd no more. You waited too long
for the sign sought for generations. The depth of the wound

didn't convince you. Only your pulsing blood reminds you that you live.
Everything else is the gift of hallucination, which leaves you unmoved:
minerals flowing in the Dinaric Alps, liver spots, mercy and the umbilical

cord. Your eyeballs quiver like a trembling poplar, and God's messenger
doesn't visit you. Nowhere to run, nowhere to hide. The whole thing
is beyond you. You just sense that grating covers the arrow slit.

Across the River, to the East

A young roebuck darts across a clearing. The ancient shot,
on a bridge in the disappearing town, reverberates through the ages.
So what. Water surges over the riverbank. The lord of corridors
tosses in a restless sleep, in the villa where the rivers meet. The empty echo

of his steps. The band in the park is ssleep. You, who survived the camps
and cold of the Urals, walk by guards who look the other way. They
flash you a secret sign. And you glide across courtyards paved with grey
bones. You crossed the last border long ago and learned the fundamental

lesson of the world: only he who accepts the painful offering survives.
Ignore the flowers' architecture! Strike as hard as he dreamed you would.
So that a skull crumbles like a vanilla biscuit on the bottom of a bowl. Strike!

So that the groans of children and angels glitter on the blade, reviving
your instincts. Let the tribe recognize itself in the wound, if there
is no other way, let it fall—that last foundation of the citadel.

The Aesthetics of Dusk

I remember the leaden breath that clouded my world. Though
not the mirrors, it's true. But I believe everyone knows that.
There's no choice. I think of the dead entering the vows
of betrothed lovers. I remember the acid rain flooding

the sidewalks and cells of the Carthusian monastery.
And I remember the bone-crushing force. It needs no verbs.
From molten lava and the silence of bystanders it shapes
a beast that darts across the fields. And enters the eternal *now*

to recognize the prey among us seated by the fireplace.
We were drawn by the will with which the somber poet changed
gender and breathed life into a monument. Who could have known

a drill of evergreen hendecasyllables would turn hope into a battlefield cry!
It's late now: a force stirs within a poem, transplanting everything
into the rhetoric of repetition, which conceals decaying forms.

The Lord of Tears

Let it be: may your ears never hear the fluttering of jackdaws
spreading over the gutters of watchtowers, like heavenly fruit. Which rots
in silence. May your steps measure the bottomless depths of the lobby
in the academy: here the breath of emissaries from distant embassies

nurtures an ancient dream. The dream of endless lands, where the same
name is spoken with the same dread. May your spit harden into crystal.
May your hand caress no one. May the heroes who crossed the Illyrian hills
and lay down in the dunes by the warm sea tell your future. Inevitably

alone. May the rising tide wash over the ruins the armies left behind.
May the commanders listen with deadly seriousness to the orders
given by memory, which thickens like wax. You'll use it

to seal up the legacy of pain growing steadily in the collected works
of the court poets. They'll flee with you to the shores of the divided
island. It will be too late when you kneel beneath a cruel star.

Second Baptism

Testament of Defeat

Are we the steam rising from the boiling cauldron or the tradition
which resists storms and the inconstancy of chieftains. Are we a line
in a musical score, a stone's lament? We know so little. In the distance
fires ignite in the eyes of our peers. We know so little. Not even

that our names have been placed on the black list. The wind whirls
across the globe, over the minarets' spires. A titmouse twitters
above the roof tiles, as it did yesterday. The moon's journey is still
the same. And us? We thought beauty's fascination and the promises

of the bards' songs echoing from hill to hill were our common property.
But that was just a saying. Because metaphors flare up in pain above the city
which doesn't empty its streets to honor the masters of evil. Like creation's

torso, we lived to hear the chant of defeat. Which we made our own.
Just as the ethics of salt and bread seemed to us a pure daily ritual.
We're as tired as the thick ash snowing through the seasons.

The Source of Oxygen

The sweet fragrance of yellow roses on the grave of the poet
who has rested for centuries in this chapel. Deer perhaps and certainly
birds will rest in your shade. And penitents are coming, following
star dust, which summons lust from naked loins. And grieving

pilgrims from harbors where no ships dare to anchor. And strangers
seduced by the glitter of a glorious past, and the source of oxygen
barely seen on the survey maps of mystics. And dandelions
growing over your pedestal, and the moonless night, and the smoke

of offerings scorching faded arabesques. I know them all. Mine
is the calendar of kneeling in a country obliterated by the future
of an illusion. Tell me, how could I not recognize myself

in the sotto voce of an elegy for orchestra and voice? How could I
not sweetly tremble in the prayer in which contempt decays?
If no one else will, I'll move my lips to keep your path forever open.

Before the Storm

The Russian hound behind the door has stopped barking. Ice floes
drift down the river. A broken toy no watchmaker will fix.
A rusty sword. The villas massed on the quay begin to wheeze.
The great river consumes them one by one, and a nun passing

through a courtyard shyly feels her way into the blue mist.
On the way home you stop to extinguish the humble light in you.
A lark warbles for a moment and then is gone. Vanished above the city
weighed down by a premonition: curses and legends aren't enough! You,

who waded through the ripples of the Jordan River, step gingerly
under the coats-of-arms turning grey on the façades. You no longer hear
a Greek mass sung at dusk. To comfort strangers and to burden you.

Your lips quiver when you pass the tyrant's tomb your grandchildren
will visit in ignorance. Tonight, like a dead guard, a young mother
stands before it, weeping. Perhaps her only child is just asleep.

Halfway to the Foreign Legion

for Francis Debeljak
Paris

Instead of you trimming hedges below an Aragon château, a stream
murmurs in remote Alpine reaches. You won't climb there again. Yet
your surprise hasn't melted. And it won't. For you gauged the depth
of vertigo and the size of the crucifix. The fire in the West stirred your hope,

and you leaped the barbed wire, and listened to the rhythm of dawns
on the edge of the Continent. You sank into a great city, where only
the inner ear counts, not the song passed down the generations.
The kindness of strangers was your morning star, the moss

on tree trunks. You weren't a visionary, just a witness to the skin
that under the occupation of the unknown rain breathes differently than
at home. Lightning mesmerized you when an angel trained his gaze on you.

You followed him, lonely, without knowing you carried the seed that would
rouse the torpid glands of servants and masters. The unchanging order
of things exhausts them. You sent me one letter. Enough to change the future.

To the Poets Exiled in Amsterdam

The scene must open with a narrow house, sleepless with the fear
of a knock at the door. And with the bed in which a child lies sobbing.
The night watch awaits a challenger. The throats of refugees
are hoarse. No word can find its way to them. And Spinoza

has locked God in polished crystals. On windy squares, wide
as the hips of caravels, the descendants of mountain lust
write their testament. Which waits for a reader. The calm furls
the sails. The skin resembles dried parchment. The only desire

they still feel: to bid farewell. Farewell to the hymn of the choir.
For every exile invents his own language. The deadly
episode in the southern ravines was brief. Yet poets stand

on the shore, protected by the law of longing. They don't care
that no one will live to see the return. And their gaze, dimly glowing
like an eternal light, rises above the uproar of the mob, dancing endlessly.

Second Baptism

for Milan Djordjević
Belgrade

The city, shaken to the bone by fear, is silent once again. Mice
sleep. No bees swarm from the hive. The uninvited guest,
like sea salt on an open wound, disappears through the open gate.
He barely had time to say goodbye to the common rooms

and the mystique of the sonnet. Noble eyes that no longer want
to see have emigrated from a family portrait. The geyser
that erupted in the middle of the park has already washed away
the son. And the mother and daughter. The hemlock potion

in their stomachs decants in bliss. The crucifix is silent, and the atlas
of the Promised Land is wrapped in darkness. We persist at home: we have
renamed wild animals and things. We are inspired by a living form,

not by the shadow stealing over the candle. The weak flame at the window
needs us: we remember every sting. That's why we endure. Like love
silently revived. Which counts no years as it ripens unrequited.

Interpretation of Love

Prayer from Pontus

If I forget you, the gift of prophesy will be lost. A wind rose
will turn wild. If you vanish like a shooting star, I will
lose my nerve and passion. Beyond the wet petals flashing
in the dark I'll go, cool as pebbles on a river bank. Pine trees

will rustle strangely, a footstep will forget how to tear itself
from the cobbled streets. The crack in the main beam of the ceiling,
which enchanted us, will close, and the light shining through it,
seducing me, will be sucked into the depths of the earth. The libraries'

last will and testament: what do I care? I live off a hidden memory,
which changes me from a hound to a wild goose. If you reveal yourself
to me for only an instant I will be truly yours. Like a tracker

who has walked barefoot all his life. I'll be a tuberose growing
through the winter, I'll be a fresco with countless layers
of gold. You are so close when you are gone.

Interpretation of Love

Two deadly beautiful fighter jets tear across the sky, and cartographers
do not rest. Time is running out. History ignites a bonfire in the bushes.
I steadfastly refuse all invitations: snowcapped Ararat, the abbey
of Aquileia, Karst stalagmites. I stand at the end of the road,

like loyalty's epilogue. Our allies' camps are far away. A plant,
not listed in any catalogue, climbs through the roof of the greenhouse.
I gaze at the anonymous temples changing in the cooling twilight.
There is no other purgatory, no other paradise. I must remain

here until all the walls are ground to flour. Then an amen
will resound so loud the last deaf bird will flinch. Grant me
strength to feel at home in my tight skin. So I can calmly pay

the dues demanded by my ancestral vault, which may be empty.
So that I, kin to the blind prophet, will recognize a familiar language
in a flower. May it open just for me when the woman I love gazes at it.

Light Above the Peninsula

You stand alone. Proud. Embedded in the ruins of the arena
Roman slaves built on a lost peninsula. Milk trickles from your
swollen breasts. Waterfalls of light cascading from the infinite
sky honor you. And we, whose arms have hardened into granite,

watch in silence. Swept off our feet by a miraculous presence.
So that we step deliberately over balconies and the honor
guard's maneuvers fill us with hope. Instead of watching
from a distance we become your guardians. Our pulse

quickens. We're keeping our ancestors' promise.
That's why we stay where we are. Easily. Without guilt.
And wait for your hand to turn us into a statue, if you like.

And we use our bodies to fortify the wall over which a foreign
gaze cannot reach. The biographies of counts and convicts
merge: we are the roof above the fruit which grows and grows.

Pula, Istria
August 1993

Night Bride

Your breath is intoxicating: fresh as an olive branch
slipped into the confessional. You are the funnel of the typhoon
that forced demons and saints to speak the same language. And lined
them up along the street. Are you coming? No, you're already here.

The migration of matter from the dead to the living means nothing to you.
You bring such terrifying beauty and unrest whirling in your orbit. As if
you don't care for the armies that follow ancient roads through the capitals.
This is our home today. Maybe tomorrow, too, if we still know how to love.

You're descending on the world, which bursts at the seams. You're
as thick as honey. Your imperative, you whisper, must be heeded:
to be. But a ghost train glides across the old continent, through

diplomatic corridors, carrying guests to a wedding. One of them is fated
to put on a crown of thorns and die. I alone will wait for all the faces
to recognize themselves in the one wrapped in translucent cloth.

Traveling to New York

for Erica

I turned my oral tradition into an endless scream.
And completed the ancestral emigration. I grew dependent
on the perfect female form. I let myself be baptized
by light, which easily revives a forgotten figure.

In which the two of us are more than the courage
which gave us life. There's nothing to hide: I breathe
so deeply the curtain in a roadside inn stirs. True,
this roof may be a temporary one. Yet here I've made

an offering of the herbs I first picked in the new world.
Long vigilance has paid off. And suddenly the course
is clear: the gift returns as the name of the child intoned

by the priests of longing. So that what multiplies in me, like endless
holograms, shall not be lost. And the distance smells of apples. I am
driven there by the lust of two, which is greater than any solitary form.

Woman's Shadow

What you implanted in my marrow I translate into a language
I haven't mastered yet: the cadence of a scream reaching
into the heart, the rumbling of an underground train, church
naves without altars, gods murmuring in the pelvis. You:

you rose from a shell like a delicate sculpture from the furnace
of a glass blower. You taught me anguish and humility
before the gospel of a demanding prophet. And the freedom
of a doe bounding across the meadows of a slumbering heaven.

I can't reach them without you. I hear the chestnuts crackling
on the terraces of my village. The asphalt is cooling. I don't care.
I'd rather tremble with delight, like a house on the verge of restoration,

when you sing a new melody. At the darkest hour of the day you show me
the alphabet of wind and fate and seeds. I read stains in history's cellar.
I know my home will be there, where you mark off the wild garden.

Young Muse

Young Muse

My ears, no, more precisely, my capillaries and body are tuned
to your cry. Gazing at an archipelago of stains on the wall,
I marvel, like Leonardo: how wide is the horizon! Bending over you,
I deliver myself to the fate pronounced by a newborn's sigh.

And a star blissfully touches me. I can't describe how tenderly
you punish me with sleepless nights, with the laurel wreath's sweet torment.
This ritual: intoxicatingly beautiful but wordless. Though I don't exist
outside verse, even I fall silent for a moment to make room for the miracle

of this day. May it never end. What was separate before you arrived
now breathes together, like a nest of quail. Fluttering fills the sky,
which isn't sinless. Yet I know: there's only one festival. I celebrate it

when you wake. The muse who removes the shadow from your cheek
comforts me, like a messenger worn down by generations. And she whispers
the name, a new source, which opens the doors to the houses of strangers.

Boundless Room

Yes, I belong to those who were once under the spell
of blood. And wild animals leaping from utopian scenes
into life to leave a mark on the hunter. And people
shaped by the age of crime and restless sleep.

I'm not saying the roar of the underground river I used
to sail attracts me anymore. I'm not saying that at all.
But the wound which condemned me to lordly solitude
has changed form. Once I was one, now I'm a tribe.

And the anguish of a boat setting off from shore inspires me
only in a mirror. I see myself only in the trembling
of a small body conjured by the sweet confusion of my desire.

I humbly praise this joy: how you show me where to receive
the gift of manna. I serve your breath redolent of milk.
I don't sleep at night so day will shine more truly.

Church Bells at Midnight

You wake up. In your own time. Like a dull red aster.
Which blooms at night, when no one's watching. Duty
and the aroma of coffee beckon me. Though I have
traversed the smooth sides of glaciers, crossed oceans,

and tied the continents together, this window is now the final
frontier. With a cautious caress I uncover your body, which glows
like silver when you turn to me. And the weight of my delight
commands me to sober up. To shed my habits. To dictate,

in a simple way, my last will and testament: for you the world will be
an open hand. No cold drafts. Memory's embers smolder forever
in a fishpond. It is you now, not me, who eagerly awaits

the new moon. And the force and subtlety of the only name I whisper
in your ear. Don't say it. Heed the footprints of sleepwalkers
while the chaos lasts. Then measure the shadow and the sky.

Gratitude

The arc of your eyebrows—so new!—draws a splendid dome
in the air. Supported by the down of the angels, the ones who guard
the doors to language. Its only rival is the grace of the silent ballerina.
Imperfect verbs: like the green snow you see now for the first time.

How it lies on a mountain range you cross in an instant. Like a comet
carrying a spark from one body to another. Your little arms embrace
the whole planet. You question the secrets of the full moon. You are
a stranger to passers-by, a gift to me: from the touch of two languages

your will grows. You take in everything, like a viaduct
boldly stretching from mother to daughter. You make
agnostics see: the sky, that quilt of lightning, is more beautiful

than a field of buckwheat. Even I'm struck. You were washed clean
when you revealed yourself to me: the eternal word. I'll admit:
I'm grateful to you for guiding me safely through the throes of birth.

Invocation by a Small Bed

The water bubbles in the radiator. And the ebb and flow of the sea
were recorded in the annals. At noon, I was absolved by the horizon.
I sense my journey is not complete. I'm just faithfully preparing
for the next task, like any father. Perhaps I'll make mistakes.

Yet the delight of discovery is sweeter than the taste
of summer's first strawberry melting on my tongue. I watch
like a treasure hunter: from your forehead I brush away the lock
of hair that upset your sisters around the world. I want more!

I want to be a crystal goblet humming under your gaze!
More disciplined than a Jesuit, I want to yearn like the gentle
breath that multiplied the wheat in our ancestral granaries.

Free of spells and doubts until my body lets me down, I want
to be like balm mint at dawn. I learn kinship's vital ties by heart.
I'm untouchable. And thrilled to learn there is no other way.

Newborn Ode

A soft baritone lifts you up, the one that drives the sap
through the neighbor's cherry tree! The lunar eclipse that covered
your forehead glorifies you! And in the cupboard a porcelain
bowl vibrates softly, like an alto sax! Cinnamon

is honored to be compared to the fragrance of your hair! When the vein
in your wrist pulses the beginning and the end of time dissolve
into a hymn of marble slabs! You grow faster than a river changing course
under bridges. You rise miraculously, like yeastless bread. When I glide

my hand over your body, smaller than a ripe fig, the sky glows.
Like fireworks. I touch the soft crown of your head, which throws
the compass needle into confusion. It opens for clarity—no longer accessible

to me. But it pours infinitely into you as from a fragile jug. Your breath
drives me to the edge. Sometimes it makes me dizzy. Yet I stand firm.
When I hold you in my arms I'm the rock from the Old Testament.

Homecoming

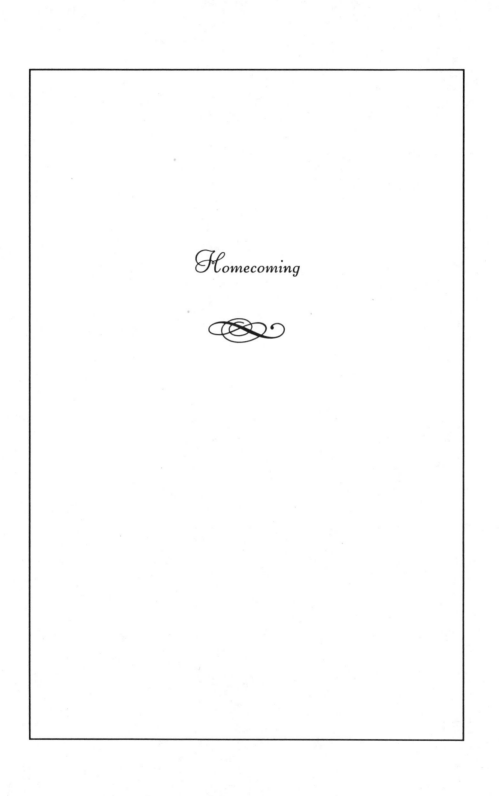

Angel on the Lake Shore

Frightened laughter on the faces of the caryatids. A captain
leaves his courtesan without saying goodbye. Waiting for him
in the sheets was a peace treaty to salve their wounds with rosemary.
He didn't pick it up. Neither did she. And I? I only register

the last note. The musicians turned into an apparition.
Overnight, the whole country sank into a crater left by a meteor.
Questions remain unanswered. Mistakes, too. Schools
of philosophy and army barracks in the bloom of May: they sank

in the pitiless dark water. The horizon can't be seen
through the surface, and a husband and wife are united only
in the liquid solitude. Once, alone, each worshiped clay idols.

Now they share their destiny with algae. I don't shed a tear.
I record what I see: a cruel star radiating from the depths,
destroying the seed that might shoot up from a common pain.

The Last Cigarette

Above the roofless library hovers a veil of smoke.
The North Star drawn sharply with a flint. With haste
I draw the smoke. I listen to a Lippizaner neighing from the depths
of an ancient ode. It came unannounced, like winter.

The hoof print on the hereditary seal is distinct. Here it is now.
Coming closer and closer. It grows, stands on its hindquarters, and
rises. It gallops into my dusk, which fell too soon. The Sava,
the Drava, legionnaires in the valley: nothing stops it. Tramping

resounds above a repentant caravan timidly making its way
to the cross and to the mountain. Simple messages might molder.
Not for me. A Marlboro burns down. I have renounced all my property.

I can feel his arrival—and the only word which will stay with me forever.
I couldn't care less if hail strikes. I know: before a shot returns me to the arms
of nothingness I'll see from my saddle an olive tree at the foot of the hill.

At the Epicenter

A spring bubbles. As if a dam broke. Yesterday it seemed
to be dying away. Yet the pressure of change is becoming slightly
cruel. There is no name for the earthquake that threw the monuments
off their pedestals. Only the muse behind the poet's statue kept her wings.

The useless speakers left. Across the border, I believe.
And the sealing wax is still smoking on the document. Confusion
reigns on the faces of the newcomers lost in the canyons between
the palaces. Of course ambition measures their hours and days. But we

are subject to another force. Each of us responds like a stone
that leafs out overnight into a tower reaching distant heights. A voice
calls us from the place where the sky meets the court of dreams.

We hear it travel like a split atom across slate, through swamps.
We are a vanishing species. An order rivets us to the ground. Nothing
moves us, neither a snowstorm aimed at us nor sand from the Sahara.

Bridge

At the place abandoned by the Praetorian Guard you'll reach
the other bank. Perfection's burden will await you there: to draw
you into its enchanted circle. Only you know how dangerous it is to pray
for the purity of form. Swallow your spit, say a word in the dialect

of the linden tree and start a new travelogue. In which the delicate
arch stretching between a brother and a sister wants to forever
reassure them. Both court the sap of a tree. To heal error's wound,
which has no mercy even for the dead. Yet the chivalrous stories stacked

in blocks on either bank make a tall mountain. At its foot
crêpe paper camps slumber, and the clock's rhythm calmly turns
darkness into dawn. History burns slowly in an urn, and the people

count the bones. How will they recognize you at all? The river
imperceptibly widens into a delta, flags flutter, and the pillars
rot. You were right: the stones piled on the banks became islands.

Boundaries of Language

for Edvard Kocbek,
wherever you are

The loom has stopped. Mushrooms give off a pleasant scent,
and a Baroque bell tolls. The rapture on the people's sweaty faces
is deeper than you know. You sing calmly. Without notes or pauses.
The limestone walls cracked in the hall your song enlarged.

Like the vault of a stormy sky before calamity. People
came to hear you, following the wolf's path across frozen lakes.
They left their spears in the yard, thick blood pooling beneath them.
You sing calmly. Landslides and floods and the death masks

of poets proclaim their secrets through you. In the hourglass, the thread
of sand has stopped. A dove has returned from a great distance,
and the ark slowly glides into the unknown. The pale sun expands

in the hearts of the masses when they hear you. For you sing to them.
A compass needle trembles: a migraine's endless wave. Pregnant women and
old men sing with you, their throats growing moist. No one can stop them.

Homecoming

A crust of thin ice cracks, and signposts change. Summer snow
slides down the Karavanke mountains. Pale princely faces. Blood
will soon return to their cheeks. The frozen woodpecker's knock
against the windowpanes awakens us. Early morning. Light teems

from cracks in the earth. What a melancholy odor rises from the boots
exhausted by the deep marsh! Above the roofs, winds from the west
and south mix, and blindness ends on the threshold of the grave. Now all
of us who left home at birth gather at this holy hour. No one needs

the broken eggshell. From its pieces emerges the map of a country defying
oblivion. In the square, the tank trap is idle again. An old woman lovingly
raises her arms, free of desire and fear. The mystery of ten days is over.

She awaits them peacefully, recognizing the despair under their helmets.
They think she's their mother comforting them. The face of a soldier old
as a Celtic vase drowns in the murmuring water that might fill the dry well.

About the Author

Aleš Debeljak holds a Ph.D. in Social Thought from Syracuse University, New York, and currently teaches in the department of cultural studies at the University of Ljubljana, Slovenia. One of the leading Central European poets, Debeljak has published five collections of poems, seven books of cultural criticism, and a translation of John Ashbery's selected poems into his native Slovenian. He was a fellow at the Collegium Budapest-Institute for Advanced Study (where most of the poems in *The City and the Child* were written) and a senior Fulbright fellow at the University of California, Berkeley. He has won several awards for his creative work, including the Slovenian National Book Award and Miriam Lindberg Israel Poetry for Peace Prize (Tel Aviv).

In addition to having poems and essays translated into twelve languages, Debeljak has published books in Croatian, Slovak, Czech, Italian, German, Hungarian, Polish, Spanish, and Japanese translation. His recent books in English include a collection of poems, *Anxious Moments*, a nonfiction volume, *Twilight of the Idols: Recollections of a Lost Yugoslavia*, and *Reluctant Modernity: The Institution of Art and its Historical Forms*. He also edited *Prisoners of Freedom: Contemporary Slovenian Poetry*, *The Imagination of Terra Incognita: Slovenian Writing 1945-1990*, and the Slovenian, Croatian, and Serbian sections of *Shifting Borders: East European Poetries in the Eighties*.

Debeljak lives in Ljubljana with his American wife and three children.

About the Translator

Christopher Merrill's books include three collections of poetry, *Workbook, Fevers & Tides,* and *Watch Fire;* the translation of Aleš Debeljak's *Anxious Moments;* several edited volumes; and three works of nonfiction, *The Grass of Another Country: A Journey Through the World of Soccer, The Old Bridge: The Third Balkan War and the Age of the Refugee,* and *Only the Nails Remain: Scenes from the Balkan Wars.* He holds the William H. Jenks Chair in Contemporary Letters at the College of the Holy Cross. He and his wife, violinist Lisa Gowdy-Merrill, are the parents of a daughter, Hannah.

THE TERRA INCOGNITA SERIES:
WRITING FROM CENTRAL EUROPE

Series Editor: Aleš Debeljak

Volume 4
Afterwards: Slovenian Writing 1945-195
Edited by Andrew Zawacki
250 pages $17.00

Volume 3
Heart of Darkness
Poems by Ferida Durakovic
112 pages $14.00

Volume 2
The Road to Albasan
An Essay by Edmund Keeley
116 pages $14.00

Volume 1
The Four Questions of Melancholy
New and Selected Poems of Tomaž Šalamun
Edited by Christopher Merrill
266 pages $15.00

POETRY IN TRANSLATION FROM WHITE PINE PRESS

PERCHED ON NOTHING'S BRANCH
Selected Poems of Attila Joszef
104 pages $14.00

WINDOWS THAT OPEN INWARD
Poems by Pablo Neruda, Photographs by Milton rogovin
96 pages $20.00

HEART OF DARKNESS
Ferida Durakovic
112 pages $14.00

AN ABSENCE OF SHADOWS
Marjorie Agosin
128 pages $15.00

HEART'S AGONY
SELECTED POEMS OF CHIHA KIM
128 PAGES $14.00

THE FOUR QUESTIONS OF MELANCHOLY
Tomaz Salamun
224 pages $15.00

THESE ARE NOT SWEET GIRLS
An Anthology of Poetry by Latin American Women
320 pages $17.00

A GABRIELA MISTRAL READER
232 pages $15.00

ALFONSINA STORNI: SELECTED POEMS
72 pages $8.00

CIRCLES OF MADNESS: MOTHERS OF THE PLAZA DE MAYO
Marjorie Agosín
128 pages $13.00   Bilingual

SARGASSO
Marjorie Agosín
92 pages $12.00   Bilingual

MAREMOTO/SEAQUAKE
Pablo Neruda
64 pages $9.00   Bilingual

THE STONES OF CHILE
Pablo Neruda
98 pages $10.00   Bilingual

VERTICAL POETRY: RECENT POEMS BY ROBERTO JUARROZ
118 pages $11.00   Bilingual

LIGHT AND SHADOWS
Juan Ramon Jimenez
70 pages $9.00

ELEMENTAL POEMS
Tommy Olofsson
70 pages $9.00

FOUR SWEDISH POETS:
STROM, ESPMARK, TRANSTROMER, SJOGREN
131 pages $9.00

NIGHT OPEN
Rolf Jacobsen
221 pages $15.00

SELECTED POEMS OF OLAV HAUGE
92 pages $9.00

TANGLED HAIR
Love Poems of Yosano Akiko
48 pages $7.50 paper   Illustrated

A DRIFTING BOAT
An Anthology of Chinese Zen Poetry
200 pages $15.00

BETWEEN THE FLOATING MIST
Poems of Ryokan
88 pages $12.00

WINE OF ENDLESS LIFE
Taoist Drinking Songs
60 pages $9.00

TANTRIC POETRY OF KUKAI
80 pages $7.00

About White Pine Press

Established in 1973, White Pine Press is a non-profit publishing house dedicated to enriching our literary heritage; promoting cultural awareness, understanding, and respect; and, through literature, addressing social and human rights issues. This mission is accomplished by discovering, producing, and marketing to a diverse circle of readers exceptional works of poetry, fiction, non-fiction, and literature in translation from around the world. Through White Pine Press, authors' voices reach out across cultural, ethnic, and gender boundaries to educate and to entertain.

To insure that these voices are heard as widely as possible, White Pine Press arranges author reading tours and speaking engagements at various colleges, universities, organizations, and bookstores throughout the country. White Pine Press works with colleges and public schools to enrich curricula and promotes discussion in the media. Through these efforts, literature extends beyond the books to make a difference in a rapidly changing world.

As a non-profit organization, White Pine Press depends on support from individuals, foundations, and government agencies to bring you important work that would not be published by profit-driven publishing houses. Our grateful thanks to the many individuals who support this effort as Friends of White Pine Press and to the following organizations: Amter Foundation, Ford Foundation, Korean Culture and Arts Foundation, Lannan Foundation, Lila Wallace-Reader's Digest Fund, Margaret L. Wendt Foundation, Mellon Foundation, National Endowment for the Arts, New York State Council on the Arts, Trubar Foundation, Witter Bynner Foundation, the Slovenian Ministry of Culture, The U.S.-Mexico Fund for Culture, and Wellesley College.

Please support White Pine Press' efforts to present voices that promote cultural awareness and increase understanding and respect among diverse populations of the world. Tax-deductible donations can be made to:

White Pine Press
P.O. Box 236, Buffalo, New York 14201